SOMEONE SOMEWHERE

An Eclectic Collection

MFON UMOREN

© Copyright 2021, Mfon A. Umoren (mau)

All Rights Reserved.

In accordance with the U.S. Copyright Act of 1976, the scanning, uploading, and electronic sharing of any part of this book without the permission of the publisher constitute unlawful privacy and theft of the author's intellectual property. If you would like to use material from the book (other than for preview purposes), prior written permission must be obtained by contacting the publisher at the address below. Thank you for your support of the author's rights.

ISBN: 978-1-948638-07-4

Cover art and design by Rafael Labrador
www.m-designz.net

To reach the author, email:
mumoren@writing.com

Also by Mfon A. Umoren

The Sound That Whispers in Me – a book of poems

Out of the Smog – spoken word cd

Blue Sad Days – spoken word cd

Barstow: An Introspective View – a novella

Table of Contents

Africa 1
Gods 2
Monochromatic Memories—Poem 3 3
Spoiled Honor 4
One 6
Star Fuckers 7
Pygmies Live 8
Death, Taxes and War 9
Guns 10
Man 11
Hannibal 12
Gvorkians 13
Hard to Forget 14
Mother and Daughter 15
Pollen 16
IOUs 17
Playthings 18
Never Maybes 19
She Said 20
Raw 21
Parts Unknown 22
A Fallen Phoenix 23
No Sidestep 25
Self-Manifestation 26
Organic 27
Hard Rain 28
A Shade of 29
Nature 30
Nebraska 31
"Thoughts" 32
Mold 33

Of Nature	34
More than Fame	35
Monochromatic Memories—Poem 2	36
In A Week	37
As It Was	38
If It Is Not Then What Is It?	39
Sunday	40
We Sat	41
Love	42
Heart Bourne	43
No Regrets	44
The Living	45
Without Novocain	46
The Blues Remains the Same	47
Global Warming	48
Inertia	49
Sane Insanity	50
On Money	51
Numbers	52
Symbiosis	53
Soft Skills	54
The Professor	55
Head West	56
California	57
Pause	58
Annabel	59
Married People	60
By-and-By	61
Cute	62
Fresh Air	63
The Red Carrousel	64
Transitory Souls	65
Predestination	66
Curiosity	67

Believers 68
Monochromatic Memories—Poem 1 69
From Clay 70
Not of Heaven.. 71
Defense Mechanisms...................................... 72
Native Sun 73
Anatomy 74
Dawn to Dusk... 75
Asia 76
Some Women.. 77
Sleeping Dogs 78
Reincarnation... 79
Live Bravely... 80
Time 82
Definitive Thoughts 83

Pygmy Intellectualism

Africa

It would be so easy to blame everything,
anything and all things on the oppressor.
It would be so vindicating inebriating to
put it all on the destroyer if it were all so true
but it is not.

Our infantile genocidal genes have proven
it all to be so damning.

We have killed our own, wasted our own
and damaged and enslaved ourselves.

It would be so easy to blame everything,
anything and all things on the molester
if we did not stop to realize that we
have been our own tormentors.

Gods

And then they came with their missiles,
bombs and rockets searing the bright blue
sky heaving thunder without rain, leaving
all our flowers dead.

And then they came with their education,
words and schools wiped the chalkboard
clean and dipped their thirsty tongues in our wells.

And then they came with their religion,
dogma and truth and told fables taller than
city towers.

They came with their wars.
They came with their words.
They came with their lust,
ate our culture in the shade,
laughed at our simplicity and
told stories as tall as city towers.

Monochromatic Memories— Poem 3

I think tomorrow I'll write my mother.
It has been awhile since the last awhile.
What will I say? "Oh…hello mother,
sorry I have not written in a while?"
No. No. That will not do, clichés, are
nothing more than recycled, dried, messages.
I think tomorrow I'll call my brother.
It has been awhile since the last awhile.
It has been some time since we last
really talked. What will I say?
"Hey bro, what's up?"

No. No. That cannot do, polite dialogue
is not, in reality, polite, now is it?
Maybe I will just hang up and feel down,
than say a trite line to begin a long banter,
in an attempt to make small conversation.

I think tomorrow I'll clean house,
throw out old artifacts, junk mail,
and shabby, tattered, faded things. As always,
I will come close to nearly finishing.
I'll stop the process, sigh, happy to
know I have made a brand new pile.

I think tomorrow I will write mother, it has
been awhile since our last long distance smile.

Spoiled Honor

Singed sod,
Slim trees,
Loquacious birds,
Bang!

Silence.
Have the feathered ones
Disappeared?
Bang!

A pained echo blast off
Sentinel hills.
Vast land, no veil.
Panting, the yellow-eyed
Ruler crouches,
Stares at the intruder.

Singed sod,
Stained grass,
Slim trees,
Quivering leaves.
Loquacious birds, no sound?

Queen-less,

Flanked by two
Shivering pawns,
Defenseless.

Hunched down,
Arched back,
Beads of sweat roll,
Roll over taut muscles.

Alone,
He declares himself,
He roars.
Bang!

Singed sod,
Slim trees,
Birds in flight.

One

A million prophets and a million saints
killed by one toy soldier.

A million fathers, a million mothers and
a million children killed by one puppet warrior.

A million years a billion tears and a zillion dreams
extinguished by a windup toy.

One million prophets and one million saints
and one toy soldier, one toy soldier.

Star Fuckers

You were not there when
top ramen was a staple
how can you ask me to go taste calamari?

You were not there when
Christmas was just another day
how can you ask me to go caroling?

You were not there when
a car seat was my bedroom
the steering wheel a living room ornament.

You were not there when
rejection was a common theme
how can its absence be so easily forgotten?

You were not there when
achievement was wrought in lonely isolation
how is it you are here on the eve of celebration?

You were not when
I was an empty shell
how can you be now?

Pygmies Live

A woman screams
A bystander dreams
A child cries
A step-father lies
An ape robs
An old man sobs

Pygmies live giants die

The poor make
The rich take
The born lend
The dead spend
Sacred land is
A well-used mound

Pygmies live giants die

Death, Taxes and War

Some people love so much,
some so little.

Some people laugh out loud,
some cry inside.

Some people get so much,
some so little.

Some people live so long,
some leave too soon.

All we have is all we have.
All we want is all we want.

Who we are is who we are.
The difference is life.

Guns

I have no allusion the spoken word can keep our animal at bay.
Boom, boom, bang, bang is what we say.

I have no delusion the written word can stay the horrors of today.
Boom, boom, bang, bang, send young Johnny to play.

I have no illusion the holy word can force the world to pray.
Boom, boom, bang, bang, mail more boys this way.

Optimistic, hopeful and wishful as an invisible being can be,
I have no vision or hallucination any word can stop our fray.

Boom, boom, bang, bang, flowing blood makes red clay.

Man

What will these womenfolk say when
they see we are just aging mortals?
What will they think when they
observe our flaws? We cry as they do.
We lust as they do. We hurt as they do
and we are as jealous as they are.
Oh Lord! What will these womenfolk
speak of when they comprehend the
aspirations of our childhood and our
present day achievements is a gap we
may not close in the days that remain?
What will they imagine when they
detect our insecurities? What will
they feel when they apprehend cinematic
heroes are pseudo caricatures of our
fantastic imagination?
But we love them just the same.
Yes! We love them just the same.
Left to their own most would not blow up villages.
Left to their own most would not manufacture
weapons of mass destruction. Left to their own
most would be like our mothers.
Oh Lord! What will they believe when they
conclude Hollywood heroes and real life men
are not blood relatives or distant cousins?
I hope they will love us just the same.
Ahh! Except, this is not the age of innocence
or of enlightenment but one of correction.
Fortunately, I surmise many of our women
do sense all I have espoused and for those
who do not and fall prey to mean-spirited men,
I sadly say to them as I conversely utter to my own kind,
you had to have passed a good man to meet a bad one.

Hannibal

In our knowledge of our worldly way
we eat to satiate our barbarianism.
And in our acquaintance of our debauchery
we dress to cover our cannibalism.

And in our experience of our past pain
we drink to inebriate what is broken in us.
And the well to do smile at the useless words of a poet
yet beckon their manservant to speak not of what is seen.

But throughout the acoustic halls of our human theaters
throughout the blue smoke bars and red truck taverns
the incessant echo of our self-deceit whispers through.

And the politician must promise more than Saint Nick
and the musician must play louder and self-medicate
to be heard. And the actress must self-destruct to negate
the contradiction of her success.

And the good doctor chooses whom to save.
And the benevolent pastor sins more than his parishioners.
And the honest banker takes more than he banks.
And the discriminated, discriminate. And the peace officer
does not keep peace.

And the dull of wit smile at the useless words of a writer
but want justice when his words come true on their block
and in their home.

And the people, two thousand years removed from Damascus,
ink themselves in protest for one does not lament on cobblestone.
And in our wisdom of our world and our way, we kill because
we cannot be and we die because we cannot live.

Gvorkians

We are afraid, we are lonely

Many cannot hear such a grand theme.

We impale ourselves with chemical daggers.

We impale ourselves in moving tombs.

We impale ourselves with cries of:

"Yes!" "Yes!"

We are afraid, we are lonely

Many cannot bear such a grand scheme.

Hard to Forget

Along the Pacific Coast Highway far from the noise and mayhem of Baal's descendants there is a place. A place not frequented by the tenants of mansions which sit on stony cliffs high above the ocean blue.

Along the windy open highway of California's Pacific Coast there is a place where I took rest and relaxation.
I met a young girl with straight white teeth and a braided lock of hair. She reminded me of a daughter I would have wanted to have.

Along the Pacific Coast Highway far from the noise and mayhem of Baal's descendants and much removed from mansions which hover above the waves of the ocean blue sea, there is a place where I took rest and relaxation. I met a thin, young, orphaned girl and could do no more than to say hello. I could do no more.

Mother and Daughter

Momma! Yes. How light does a black person have to be to pass for white? Pretty light dear. Pretty light.

Momma. Yes dear. If a person is really, really, light won't she know she is black? Not always honey, not always.

Momma. Uh-huh. What color am I? You are caramel-colored dear. Is that really, really, good or really, really, bad momma?

It is very, very, good dear. Mr. Johnson our grocer sells your flavor all day long. He sells your bittersweet flavor all day long dear.

Momma. Yes. Can I go outside? Just for a bit honey dinner will be ready real, real, soon.

Pollen

Help one to read
Help one to write
Help one to see

And the spore will blow with the breeze

Help one to dare
Help one to share
Help one to care

And the spore will sail with the wind

Help one to eat
Help one to exist
Help one to engender

And the spore will pollinate

Help one to articulate
Help one to postulate
Help one to educate

And the spore will disseminate

Help one to inseminate
Help one to impregnate
Help one to germinate

And the spore will float in the sky

Help one to help more

IOUs

Some women say they want a male companion
when all they really want is to hear their father's voice.

And some men say they want a committed love
when what they really need is a sexual liaison.

Are you borrowing me or am I borrowing you?
Are you using me or am I abusing you?

I tell you what you want to hear.
You show me what you need me to see.

Some women say they want a strong man
when what they really want is a compliant one.

Some men say they want a homemaker when what they should
say is they need a bread maker who will stay at home.

Are you borrowing me or am I borrowing you?
Are you loving me or am I destroying you?

Playthings

am I a toy?
toys get discarded
when torn.

am I a gadget?
gadgets get used
broken and abused.

am I a trinket?
trinkets get put aside
when newer shinier
playthings emerge.

Never Maybes

The radio is off stirring air is my surround sound.
I am not speeding, just moving fast enough to get to
where I want to go but slow enough to take a long
look out of the window.

How sad I feel to drive along a country road and
see a deserted, crumbling home. I think, at one time
this was someone's pride and joy. At one moment
in time, someone had dreams for this place.

How sad I feel to drive along a one lane side road
and witness the empty remnants of someone's
life.

Driving along a one lane country road reminds me
once again why I seldom listen to the blues or a Nashville song.

The air is off and the windows are down. I am not
speeding, I am just going fast enough to get to
where I want to be.

She Said

She said tell me something nice. At her behest,
I said, "Dear there are flowers in the world
and those who are apt to smile see their budding beauty
living between the rocks."

In a moment when we were not alone in our thoughts,
she said, tell me something nice. At her request,
I said, "Love there are flying birds in the sky and those
who are apt to cry see their flapping wings soaring
through the storm."

In the quiet solitude before dawn, she whispered tell me
something. I said, "I work so I can walk up a mountain.
I walk so I can run under a cloud and I run because I was once a child."

Raw

A moment ago you forced yourself out of bed. You forced yourself to shake off your need to sleep. Get it on paper, get it down and done it is literary coercion or a jamming in of something which does not fit. You know tomorrow's woe will suppress today's foe.

The day began with your lover saying, "I am not a gold digger and you do not have any gold." She is a good woman whose ears hear everything you say but revises, edits and censors her own words.

A moment ago you tried to read Morrison to relax after hearing Al Young. Now you force yourself to put your thoughts to pen and paper all to inscribe an emotional experience that will surely leave an indelible yet invisible welt on your back.

Over the years you have accumulated a few. Over time these whip marks have fused and become rivers running through your dark brown skin, canals that carry sweat from your nape all the way down to the bottom of your spine.

Every now and then a nonchalant word or a vile look will form a blister. It will fester then pop and bleed a filmy, sticky pus and this gooey fluid will merge with the sweat current coursing down the invisible rivers life wounds have furrowed on your back.

The day began with your lover saying you are poor; it got better when you heard a man of letters speak. A moment ago you pushed away sleep. You forced yourself to get it down and done.

You know tomorrow's woe will replace today's row and you hope when these words are read, a little more wealth will come to those who are poor and even more to those whose murky tides are invisible to a lover's eye.

Parts Unknown

A man named Bourdain, a famous painter, an acclaimed writer,
a pop culture musician and on the hour and around the clock,
a neighborhood kid down the block.

A self-inflicted self-harm genocide as deadly as a napalm spray of pesticide.
A gunshot, a train hop, or a pill pop does it even matter?
The end nullifies the means.

Faced with such dire news we scream our abject ire. Why!

A handgun wound, a drug overdose, a dangling body.
Still wondering why, we say, they were too tired,
had experienced too much pain and had
seen enough hard rain.
That's why they took their own lives to parts unknown.

For those of us left behind who are placed in such mire,
there is a great amount of resentment.

Dude, lover, friend, brother, sister or dad, why did you do that?

The outrage felt by those left behind are for many reasons.
In our internal analysis we come to a shocking conclusion,
our anger is because we let them in.

We let them in our private lives.
We let them in our private thoughts.
We shared with them what we personally owned.

We would not have given them a part of us
if we knew to them we were not that significant,
to them we were just transitory souls and
despite our love for them, they would ultimately
take their own lives to parts unknown.

A Fallen Phoenix

Dwellers of this volatile sphere,
aren't we deeply touched when awakened
and shocked with news of a pre-mature loss?
We sigh and moan, asking why?
"Why Lord, why him, why her?
They were so young and oh-so beautiful".
We ought to address ourselves,
not the sky above.
Whom best to answer but we,
the architects of outcry?

Reflection manifest that
only through tragedies
will we be reminded, nothing,
absolutely nothing, on this earth
is avowed, except death. But in life,
everything and anything is conceivable.

Have not the ill deeds of eon's eluded time?
Senescent plays revived by their originator's progenies.
Transcend past the realization of self-destruction,
beyond paralytic knowledge. Behold for one hero mourned,
there are hundreds who've suffered quietly,
thousands who have violently died.
Millions who've endured torture and malady,
never once hearing woes of sentimental pacifism,
nor felt salt droplets on neglected wounds.

"Who are they, silent martyrs?"
They are kin, brothers, sisters, mothers,
and fathers carved from the same bone.
They live and perish among us,
an end without fanfare.
Their demise, the result of man's
manufactured affliction, isn't heard.

A tamed passing unlike our heroes
whose self-inflicted fatality
is publicized catastrophe.
We eulogized the glorified,
tributary offerings for a celebrated few
who seem to seldom want life.

No Sidestep

Embrace it
Adore it
Relish and
Cherish it
There is no
Getting around it
There is no free pass
There is no escape

Embrace it
Adorn it
Yield and
Succumb

There is no absolution
And resolution
From the good and bad
Emotions that comes
From living, loving
And dying

What is to be is to be

Self-Manifestation

Do not bring to fruition
an intuitive fear
see the ones already here.

Do not manifest a repetitive
sorrow when there are
so many to borrow.

Do not in mind or sight
bring to view a
somnambulist brew.

Do not conjure evil or
ensure destruction when
summer flowers are in construction.

Do not dare the dead to appear
when the bright leaves of fall
are soon to disappear.

Do not utter a woeful incantation
when nature's beauty lives in a
hopeful imagination.

Do not in mind manifest
what does not exist
leave that to those other
bizarre people.

Organic

Open dry landscape
tumble weeds rolling by
a deserted old truck
resting on cement blocks.

The scene reminds me that
yesterday's memories will
always be yesterday's thoughts.

And the somber picture I see
today is the reality from the
culmination of all my
yesterdays.

Hard Rain

It comes hard and unexpectedly and we suddenly
remember our human frailty. With wide eyes,
we scamper into our assorted shelters
some with grace and others with less nobility.

It comes fierce and unrelentingly aggression with no
bias we circumstantially consider our mortality.
Then without the influence of man or by the collateral charm
of a woman, it subsides leaving no doubt our rule and
existence is marked not by the hand of divinity.

In the distant gray sky, there is light ebbing through. Some meekly and others
with more grandiosity, we the children of Baal, emerge from our habitats.
Adorn in our raiment of class we mount our chariots blaring trumpets in our
campaign to reclaim that which was never ours.

It comes hard and unexpectedly and we suddenly
remember our human frailty. With wide eyes,
we scamper into our assorted sanctuaries
some with grace and others with less religiosity.

A Shade of

Perhaps we are like the spectrum colors of a rainbow.
In the beginning when we are young and innocent,
and closer to the ground, we are a wisp of light yellow.
As we mature, age and gather inert brown debris maybe we
grow darker and move through optical moods of red,
orange, green, blue and violet hues.

Perchance we are indeed like the diverse colors of a rainbow.
When we are young, pure of heart and sound, our air is bright.
And as we mature, age and release moisture from sorrow and
toil our nature becomes darker.

Maybe we are only rainbows and maybe we all embody the full
spectrum of life and our differences and our misunderstandings
is nothing more than the transient shade of a new color.

Nature

After the Anger Has Quieted

outside in the peaceful air of a sea front cottage
amid the sound of ocean against shore
I hear a seagull's mating call.

After the Rage Has Dissipated

deep in the timber rich valley of the sun
amid the cries and echoes of the forest's wild
I see a small clearing.

After the Self-Wounds Have Healed

inside the four walls of my domain
before the time of somnambulation
dancing between the lobes of my cortex
I am aware of that which has escaped me.

After the Anger, the Rage and the Self-Inflicted Wounds

have healed. I learn not to denigrate that which has
eluded me. Deep in the valley of the sun, amid the glow
of a crescent moon, and among the cries of the wild, I am naked.

Nebraska

A plain
flat state.
Ordinary inhabitants
live smooth
level lives –
not interested
in rocky
wooded boundaries
that extend
beyond their
even condition,
but bemused
by an
unchanging habitat.

"Thoughts"

I saw a movie where it was said,
"The silence that reigns in a cemetery
is unlike any other silence."

And I thought the emptiness that
exist in thin air is as empty as
silence is silent.

I saw a news show where it was
reported a man was so distraught
he set his children, his home and
himself on fire.

And I thought as a race what we
kill, murder and destroy is always
the leading story.

I sat and thought these thoughts
in the noisy mayhem we call a
shopping mall and I smiled at the
horde who walked by.

Mold

You get out of bed like an over-fed dog wobbling to food. You do not need an alarm; life's normal has synchronized your routine. You take a leak and recall the time your prof lectured on how morning squirt is yellower than afternoon piss. He used the word sallow, you do not care if yellower is even a word; it is the release and flow that counts. You move to the kitchen and make a cup of dope and go back to the bedroom to choose what to wear. Will it be an Old Navy khaki with a light blue shirt or will you attack the day hard, like cold, cool, Johnny Cash?

You sip your black brew and for a moment, ponder the different forms of screw in the end settling on the one a person needs the help of another to do. Finally you get dressed and eventually get to your car and on your trip you think how much has changed since those years when books were your shelter from reality and this thought steers in the idea you have always admired and taken a fancy to anything not pseudo. You park and head to your cubicle and in the process wonder, whether you turned off the coffee pot?

Of Nature

Many like rain and gray skyline shadows
as for me, a drizzle or even a light April shower
reminds me of heavy tears. Some like four seasons
something new they reason. As for me,
autumn wind is a lost child, winter snow
a synonym for an isolated soul and an early
spring breeze, smells of camphor and tragedy.
Sunny, warm, and mild keep it even keel I say.
A number like animals that slither and hiss,
sniff and huff and scratch and bark, as for me,
I would much rather cuddle and nuzzle with a
Homo sapient. More than a few like noise,
the crowd, the hustle, the bustle, the yells, and the shrieks
and loud horns of humanity. As for me, I like my day
to go like the tick and tock of a good Swiss clock.
A smile, a handshake and a friendly serenade
would suit me just fine. Many like rain and an overcast hue
as for me, it reminds me of the things I will never do.

More than Fame

Birds are chirping in the trees - some flying on
and around the limbs. I do not care to know their names
seeing they are beautiful is more than knowing the same.

White, puffy clouds are hanging in the morning sky.
I do not care to know their type, seeing they are wonderful
is more than winning any trivia game.

The sun is smiling through the stratosphere.
I do not care to know if the weather will be fair,
soon enough, there will be plenty to bear.

Birds are chirping in the trees, white, puffy clouds are
floating in the sky and the sun is shining bright –
for me – this is more than any human can claim.

Monochromatic Memories— Poem 2

There are moments when my thoughts are not preoccupied with absorbing fragmental pieces of the day. There are episodes when a complete valuation of my life is the work of my mind.

In these times of deep reflection, a persistent contemplation is: "Whatever happened to me?" I must say this morose form of speculating was not present in the sunny years of my youth. I surmise it is wrong to presume yet I would declare the desire to resolve my query is the lord of my thoughts and perchance this is also true for those whose bodies and minds have lived beyond the ideals of their adolescence.

There are minutes when my thoughts are not occupied with absorbing fragmental bits of the day, occasions when the life I have lived is the task of my mind. In these spells of deep deliberation, I wonder if age has changed me and I ponder if the successive years of discontent is my ailment, the disease that has chipped my character as a sculptor chips a block of stone.

There are moments, a quiet space in an ordinary day, when I examine the life I have lived.

In A Week

Men are this and men are that, black men the worst
I listened, nodded and bought two books from a
female author, did an interview with the feminist
and loaded her author's profile on my site.
Men are this and men are that, black men the worst
I listened, nodded and sought a reciprocal look from a
separatist. It did not come. Knowing no one is one
hundred percent right one hundred percent of the time,
and realizing at this point in my life, I have nothing left but honesty,
I packed up my agreeableness and returned home to what I knew,
watched a game, and waited to go out with a younger woman
who does not read but is a much better fit. Men are this and men are that,
I did not disagree and I did not care to tell the dramatist,
the gift to our craft is to write to the tip but not depart from the truth.
Men are this and men are that, black men are the worst. I listened,
nodded and told a younger woman it is not her fault or a sin
that she can cook.

As It Was

As it was before the millennium,
the passion, tenderness, and intimacy
we commuted were as authentic as
my need to find work.

As it was, the heroes and lovers who
preceded our cohabitation were as
numerous as the meals we shared.

As it was before the New Year,
the passion, tenderness and intimacy
we commuted did not indicate
you or I would leave.

As it was a year ago, a month ago or
as it is a moment before, affords no
assurance a lover's cause will continue.

If It Is Not Then What Is It?

Though you did not love me as I loved you,
I knew your flaws were attributed to manmade laws.

Though you did not admire me as I revered you,
I knew your ways were perpetuated by a nudge or a sway.

And though you did not see me as I saw you, with unashamed embarrassment and tribulation, I relished your short stay.

Knowing despite my open obsession you would one day go away.

And I all too well know, when you have traveled, experienced and conceived, I will not be the same person you deceived.

Sunday

Leaning back on the couch, sipping my second cup of coffee,
I stare through my lover's large, sliding glass door. Her roses,
yellow and red are blooming. Her chives, oregano, parsley,
rosemary and thyme herbs are hung over but will soon rise to the sun.

I finally let her stray cat in. He's taken to stretching his claws on
her rust colored leather sofa. She does not mind the scratching
as much as I do. Addicted to my morning habit, I have been up
for a while, she is still sleeping.

Contemplating nothing but yet pondering, I gaze outside at
the light and dark green foliage moving with the daybreak
breeze. I have not decided whether I will make it a church day.
I want and need spiritual guidance but do not care for the fat
that comes with a minister's meat and potatoes sermon.

Relaxing on the couch, enacting my dawn ritual of speculating.
I wonder about the emotional and collateral damage of losing out
on another job. I think about making it a church day. I think about
going to sunrise worship but sensing, this week, I am all prayed out.

In between a sip of coffee and after a thought, I look out through
my lover's large, clear, sliding glass door. Her plants are waving
in the wind. Her orphan cat is eating in the kitchen. She is still
sleeping but her roses are blooming.

We Sat

We sat in silence but spoke volumes.
We sat in silence and exchanged our
coronet of thorns. We sat in a colorless room
walked by matrons in padded white shoes.
We sat in the quietude of an angry gray day.
We sat in silence and shared our grief.
We sat in silence separated by a wreath.

Love

It can stay hunger and
endure misery and pain.
Shepherds found it in
a manger and history is
made for those slain
in its name. The poor are
born with it and the rich
must pay for a bit.
Love, they say, can
bear all that we fear.

Heart Bourne

Without love it is so easy to catch the flu,
so simple to get a head cold, a breeze to
feel a shiver. Without love, it is easy to
catch pneumonia, simple to get influenza,
a breeze to feel a hot fever. Without love,
it is easy to catch an infection, simple to
ache and twinge, cough and sniffle,
and be congested with phlegm.
Without love it is a cinch to catch your death.

No Regrets

I did not know what you wanted,
to hug, kiss and cuddle or to wake
in our housecoats and saunter around
in our slippers spreading homemade
marmalade on slightly tanned toast?

I did not know what you wanted,
to hug, kiss and cuddle or to lay
side by side with our differences
separating us, enacting our own
bundling love?

I did not know what you wanted,
but I tried to understand the custom
of unmarried couples.

I did not know what you wanted,
but I tried to appreciate our routine.

The Living

The holidays come like birth, age and death without our consideration.
The lonely elaborate merriness and the unhappily married chatter away
like sorority sisters in a coed dorm.

Christmas comes like rain, wind and sun without our concession.
The lonely fabricate joyfulness and the unhappily betrothed chatter away
like magpies in a storm giving witness they are not alone.

The New Year comes like fall, winter and spring without our voice
and the lonely and the unhappily living, pretend serenity.

Without Novocain

All the way to the hilt
sliced down to the bloody tip
I have seen horrible faces
smelled pungent feces
and walked through razorblade fields.

Hold the gin and leave out the tonic
I will plunge all the way in and feel
my sins rippling through my brown skin.

All the way to the bloody bone
no damper no mediator or conciliator
solitude confinement for this lonely prisoner.

I have seen our contemptible faces
smelled our disease laden excrement
and walked through our glass ridden fields.

Thanks no, hold the materialistic apparition,
stay the mindless capitalization, I'll see,
taste, touch, and take life's medicine undiluted.

The Blues Remains the Same

Surviving in a Twenty-First Century inner city
ain't far from living as a backwoods sharecropper
in the Nineteenth Century.

The guitar strumming cuts and chases
straight bourbon and you sing another
Love Song for Bobby Long.

Surviving in a Twenty-First Century city
ain't that far from living in a Nineteenth
Century slum. Time changed but the people stayed.

The piano keys cuts and chases Old Yeller
and the moonshine and you play another
Love Song for Bobby Long.

No sir, playing the blues in the city ain't
any prettier than singing it in the Delta.
Time changed but the people stayed.

Global Warming

They say there is no collusion
between rising verbal pollution
and environmental disillusion.

They say there is no collusion
between spewing human hatred
and enabling genocidal fascination.

They say there is no collusion
between a populist uprising and the
demise of a downtrodden minority.

They say there is no collusion
between global warming and the
swarming of houseflies and lies.

Inertia

She walks by with oscillating hips and I think
of how her gait takes oxygen from her mind.

He strolls by with an air of superiority and I think
of how many underpaid actors there are.

She ambulates by with a delicate scent and I think of
how alluring her fume would be if she smelled of sweat.

He foots by with bombastic noise and I think
of how profoundly powerful the quiet are.

She walks by, he strolls by and I prance by and I think
of how many of us do not get to where we want to go.

Sane Insanity

It does not surprise me the things you and I wish for,
they are not that different. One day of bliss, a firm embrace
or a sensuous kiss. A day different from all the bland,
blended rest. I cannot speak for you but for me, I need more
than the breathing and the living of a repetitive past.

The same song, the same movie, the same food and the same
drive home – and I wonder how soon it would take you or me
to grow weary of the new.

I cannot speak for you but for me, I see the benefit of children
in a long life span, they add novelty to our recycled,
regurgitated lives.

Maybe I should have lived well in the past when death came
before boredom yawned or maybe I should come well in the
millennium when speed and the stars will be our seed.

Alas my anthem of grief is but a reminder of an era when
song came from vinyl and we moved to skip a monotonous beat.

No, it does not surprise me the things you and I wish for, they are
not too different. One day of bliss or an embrace and a soft kiss.
A time apart from all the bland blended hours.

On Money

In this world there is much more fluff
than there is tangible stuff but I do not mind,
the republic can also serve the public.

In some neighborhoods there are more
nannies than there are children with
sore fannies, but I do not mind, owning
ten cabbage patch dolls does not mean
we will live without a scratch.

In this world there is more injustice
than there is just but I do not mind,
I see the same sky, the same ocean
and I smell the same rose as the privilege do.

In our world there is so much more
than one person could ever hope to buy
and so much more fluff than tangible stuff.
But I do not mind, I do not mind.

Numbers

A young teen trying to leave family
and heritage behind works the cash register.
He hits the wrong keys and a customer walks
out with thirteen extra dollars. The door closes
to the sound of next.

A night shift custodian sees a supervisor
two decades his junior, he says a humble hello.
The young boss man calls him by another name and
the door closes to the sound of a vacuum.

A five and dime owner running his mom
and pop store shoos away four neighborhood thugs
but not before one takes what they came to get for free.
And the door closes to a chorus of profanities.

A single-mother of three tries her best not to look like
the other single mother's of three. She calls to check
on her kids and hopes this time, this one, will not see
desperation in her eyes. And the door to her
private room opens too soon after dinner.

A bookish schoolteacher wakes to the static sound
of channel twelve gone off the air. He drinks a cup of tap
water and leaves the dinner dishes where they are and enters a
bed he never needs to make and his eyes close to a white
room of dreams.

A patrolman driving his beat stops to ask a shade tree mechanic
if he has seen so and so, the mechanic wipes his hands and takes
a look at six photos. He shakes his head and hands the pictures
back. The cop closes the door to his patrol car and slowly drives
away wondering if it is the twentieth or the twenty-seventh
he has the kids.

Symbiosis

We have gone through some wars
and though I may not have fought
a battle, I have felt it.

We have gone through some death
and though I may not have died
I feel dead.

We have gone through some pain
and though I may not have experienced
it, I still winced.

We have gone through some separation
and though I was not the bride or bridegroom,
I am divorced.

We have gone through some turbulent times
and though I am not the twin of trouble,
I am not the identical person I should be.

Soft Skills

When I take a chance and tell that I write,
a smile comes on the man of brawn's face.
No, I imagine words do not build real bridges
nor do they erect sturdy skyscrapers.
In our fictional world, sandy hair and a square jaw
does all of that.

When I take a chance and say that I cry,
a smile appears on the man of bronze's face.
No, I imagine masculine emotion is not a
virtue to a warrior's badge of courage.

When I take a chance and show vulnerability,
the lion and the lioness look up from their drinking hole.

The Professor

Sometimes a blazer, colder months a cardigan, but many times
a well-worn corduroy. On sweltering summer days, a loose,
white shirt, khakis and old Birkenstock sandals.

Arms behind his back, he paces as he lectures, walking the aisles,
climbing the hall steps, and he stops on occasion to let his words
settle to the ground like soft, wet, snow falling on a dark, winter night.
When satisfied that one of his students has heard something, he continues.

At times a blazer, grayer seasons a cardigan, but most often
a well-worn corduroy. Arms behind his back, he paces as he lectures,
striding the aisles and mounting the lecture hall steps and on occasion
while still speaking, he momentarily departs his human form.

He wanders from his spoken words and reflects on what more he can say
and while still speaking he aborts an unfinished sentence and allows
the silence to settle to the ground like soft, wet, snow falling on a dark,
blue night. When satisfied that one of his students is aware, he says,
"Everything we know was once just a dream."

Head West

In the heartland,
It is not enough to know.
It is not enough to show
Sense. Nor is it
Enough to reveal real
Currency. No, even that
Does not assure the
Bronze commonality.
Hence, I left.
Not in shame,
Nor with blame.
I left for a seashore.
Here, way out here,
Fame is the same
As a provincial name,
It cannot be ignored.

California

Sunday into Monday
like flowing fluid
spreading on fabric.

You sleep, but are you sleeping?
You work, but are you working?
You eat, but taste nothing.

No reason, no season,
everyone is beautiful,
everyone is someone.

Heat is haze,
smog is fog,
today was yesterday
and tomorrow is today.

In a state,
you came for a change,
found it more of the same.

The tan native a vegetarian,
his mate a decoration,
their whelping newborn,
tumbles and stumbles –

easy prey yelping
in the Mediterranean sun.

Pause

It occurs in the middle of living life,
it transpires in the transient in between of
somnambulating, being occupied, and in the exertion
of thinking of doing something. It is in the quietude,
calmness and stillness of this momentary, fleeting time
when we are not distracted or inebriated that we become
fully aware of that which we must do.

Annabel

Dark auburn mane, a sanguine smile,
with her lithe opaque hand, blue veins
showing through, a tributary of blood
flowing to her fingertips, she knocks on
doors carved from ancient wood. Once inside
she only sees a vaulted ceiling. Standing erect,
black stockings running from her hips to her toes
with a coquette voice and bony fingers she taps
on mansions owned by men. Once inside
she only sees the wealth looking up.

Married People

"I'm coming." He groaned into the receiver.
"You just got in!" Scolded his wife.
"I'm sorry dear, it's the job."
I'll be back in shortly."
He said quietly slipping - out.

By-and-By

I am not estranged to fate though
she has been a hard mate to date.
I am not foreign to love though
my mind has yet to discern the gift
from above. I am not a novice
to vice or the things which are nice
one or two have clung to me like lice.
I am not a stranger to pain it is a
reoccurring theme I have gained
again and again. I am not a virgin
to life on occasion I have explored it
as thoroughly as a husband enjoys
his wife. I am not a guest to fate
though she has been a hard mate to date.
I have been told through winter's frost
and during summer's scorch her
unforgiving highness waits upon
those who are late.

Cute

In the throes of an early dawn caffeine and nicotine fix,
I tell a friend she is cute. And I tell you; it is better to be cute than beautiful.
Cute is approachable, cute is adorable, cute is comfortable,
cute unlike a beautiful
car, may not have a million miles of wear and tear.

Under the influence of sleep, I say what I would edit later in the day,
I tell a friend she is cute. And I tell you; it is better to be cute than beautiful.
Cute is functional, cute is practical, cute is pleasurable, cute unlike a beautiful
woman, may not have a million miles of wear and tear.

In the throes of my early dawn caffeine and nicotine fix,
I share with a mate a truth about men, we do not marry women who
remind us of our mothers because we need infant care, we marry such women
because they provide the warmth, the happiness and the security we lost
when we left our maker's side.

Under the influence of an awakening state,
I say what I would conceal later in the day,
I tell a woman what many men do not share;
we are attracted to and yet frightened by
women who think we are good when we are not always,
we are infatuated by women
who believe in us when we often do not believe in ourselves,
we are made crazy by
a she who loves us unconditionally.

Fresh Air

When I think of my one great love,
I do not imagine hectic holidays
with over-bearing relatives and
screeching children. I fantasize
on the places I have never been to.
I think of open-air vacations,
mountainous regions, gondolas and Venice,
cafes in Paris, rainbow colors and spring seasons.

When I think of my one great romance
and the love of a woman, I do not
imagine sensational excursions with
roaring crowds and blaring horns.
I fantasize on the places I have never
been to. I think of outdoor vacations,
scenic seas, green pastures and the hue
of a setting sun.

When I think about my one great love,
I do not imagine the tragedies that
has befallen other lovers. I picture one
woman, one place and one moment.

The Red Carrousel

The candy apple merry-go-round stood out on the Kansas plain
evening coming sooner after the wheat harvest,
more folks were climbing out
of their flat boards touching their bib over-all pockets
before their dusty boots
hit the ground. In these first name only parts,
money like this fair came once a year.
A piece away the men folk and a few hands were gawking it up,
playing games
men who are not accustomed to fun or money play.
The candy apple merry-go-round
went round and round with a blond-headed little girl
sitting straight on her unicorn
horse.

A pace away the men were funning but next to the carousel
with the light-headed girl, it was unnaturally quiet.
I heard the wheel's music more in my head than in my ear.
When the ride stopped she got off with the help of her kinfolk
and took a crutch that helped her one leg walk.
Evening coming an hour sooner after the harvest
and more and more folks jumping off their flat boards,
I did not get to see if the little missus had blue eyes,
watching her hobble away, I reckon she'd seen enough
to have nothing but pretty blue eyes.
The candy apple merry-go-round stood out on the Kansas plain
going round and round into the night.
A family of women did their best to get back on their wagon
that brought them to
a fair with a red carrousel.

Transitory Souls

Two souls sharing a ride, he wishes he had a better
nine to five. She desires a newer man and their cabbie
thinks about a quickie with Lucille who lives on Broadway.

— and they can almost hear the music whispering through —

Two souls sharing a ride, he wishes he could spend more
time with a son he inherited. She hopes the holidays would
just come and go and their cabbie thinks about calling Lucille.

— and they can almost hear the music whispering through —

Two souls living fraternal twin lives he stares out
one window and she the other, transitory images flash and
swirl past them. Some pictures stay, squeezed between persistent thoughts.

— they can almost hear the music whispering through—

Two souls sharing a ride, he wishes he had a better
trade. She desires a newer team and their cabbie
wonders whether he fed the cat.

— on a warm, breezy, summer night, with the windows down,
they can almost hear, they can almost hear the music whispering through—

Predestination

We are born in the day, night and in the cold.
We are born to the black, brown, yellow and white poor.
We come with filled lungs screaming a cry of old.
We emerge raw and pure from our mother's door.

We are found in the stone halls of a mansion.
We are found on the bare floors of a plantation.
We are found in the gloom of an institution.
We are found in the gray rooms of destitution.

And we grow from that which we are asked to bear.
And we grow from that which we are asked to suffer.
And we grow from that which we are asked to fear.
And we grow from that which are the sins of lovers.

And we live in a world not of our creation.
And we work from an empty heart's obligation.
And we long for a place free of persecution.
And we dance in a trance of self-mutilation.

We are born in the day, night and cold air.
And we who shun our station are met with a glare.

Curiosity

When we have drunk all the spirits
there is to drink, we will be less thirsty.

When we have sexed those we want to sex,
we will be less anxious.

When we have bought all there is to buy,
we will be less greedy.

When we have eaten all there is to eat,
we will be less hungry.

When we have failed, failed and failed again,
we will know we have no other hand to play.

When we have drunk, sexed, bought, and eaten
enough and when we have opened all the doors,
we will see, behind a closed door, is an empty room.

Believers

A starched-neck minister finishes his sermon with a resounding amen.
Later, at home, in his attic he leafs through a different book.

A bespectacled grade school teacher shakes hands after her conference.
Later, at home, she presses against a full-length mirror aroused,
naked and ashamed.

A middle-aged woman wearing too many rings on too chubby fingers sops
up the last of the Alfredo sauce. Later, at home, she cuddles with her cat.

A curly-haired little girl lies awake in a fetal position, clutching teddy.
Later, in her quiet home, her father will snore next to her,
teddy thrown against the wall.

A homeless, slender lad stands on a corner looking for a few friends.
Later, much later, in the night he will meet one in the john.

A handsome man finds comedy in all things.
Later, after morning exercise, Vivaldi echoing through his home,
his doctor tells him something that brings no smile.

An unemployed immigrant stalk's an invisible job. Later, in a one room flat,
he tells his sick mother there is no work and there is no money.

A busy wife passes out protest pamphlets.
Later, after her day's march, she rushes
home to make dinner for her husband who takes his naps in the attic.

Monochromatic Memories—Poem 1

They tell me pain is pain
then why does it hurt me
more to see a dirty crying child
than a homeless hungry man?

They tell me life is life
then why does it tear me
so to see a pregnant woman's strife
than the old hang on to life?

They tell me death is death
then why does it torment me
more to see a little coffin lowered
than a large one carried?

They tell me beauty is beauty
then why is it that those who
truly are the sweetest are the
last to be call pretty?

From Clay

I cannot say that being a father is nothing
when men seek only to see their sons gather.
I will not say that being a mother is barren
when women live only to hear their
names uttered. I should not say there is
more good than evil when those who sing
at a revival are the same ones who
defy the bible. I would not say that
yesterday will be today and today
will be tomorrow when all our deeds is
a price those born of clay all have to pay.

Not of Heaven

She stands drained of all that is dead.
Afraid, appalled and aghast at our twisted,
contorted faces.

Hovering above the blood drenched fields
seeping into the rice stalk which no holy man
has sown enough to feed our hunger,
she sheds a tear for our killing, our burning
and our raping.

She stares emptied of all that is red.
Aware, amazed and annoyed at our twisted,
contorted lives.

Hovering above the corpse filled groves which no
holy man has found enough souls to harvest,
she says a prayer for our shooting, our bombing
and our looting.

She opens her wings and slowly turns, smiles
when she sees a suspended leaf, held and
gently rocked by her father's invisible hand.

She ascends drained of all that is human.
Afraid, appalled and aghast at our twisted,
contorted, race. She spreads her wings and
soars thinking, what from earth, is from heaven?

Defense Mechanisms

Please, please, do not project
your idiosyncrasies on me,
I adorn no earrings.

Please, do not interject
your gender issues on me,
I use enough of my own tissues.

Please, please, do not distort
your hate on me, it is a musty,
old recourse of finding a scapegoat.

Please, do not sublimate
your own desires on me, if you missed
the train, catch the late one.

Please, please, do not project
your own craziness on me,
it is just an ego form of laziness.

Native Sun

For those of us who have been shamed, it was
our name not our will that was claimed.
To those of us who have been violated, it was
our skin and not our spirit that was desecrated.
For those of us who have died, it was
our corpse and not our soul that perished.
To those of us who have been blamed, scorned,
torn, worn, wronged and defamed, it was
our body and not our heart that was tamed.

Anatomy

Much can be told from our eyes,
our sorrows, our difficult miles
and the crowfeet from our lies.

So much can be seen in a face,
our race and even our social place,
harden etched lines from disgrace.

Much can be learned from the mouth,
our town of birth or whether we
dwelled north or south of the tracks.

So much can be read in our hands,
a manicured life of work or the
callous from unmet plans.

Much can be told from our eyes,
the crowfeet from the lies of yesteryear
or the gleam for tomorrow's New Year.

Dawn to Dusk

Agreeable or nay we cannot
Stay yesterday though the tears
We shed remind us that sorrow
Is the soul's marrow

Favorable or not
Today is a reflection of our
Past days a solemn reminder
Of what is right and what is wrong

Good or bad pleasurable or naught
We cannot change yesterday
Tomorrow will be tomorrow
And the lark will wake with a song

Asia

She asked, "Have you ever
dated someone like me?"
I thought for a moment
and said, "I want honesty,
intelligence and substance.
Many times you do not get
that in the color and size
you desire." She stared at me
for a while, laughed and said,
"Poetic words from a poet."
I looked at her, smiled and
told her, "A failed tryst or two
has taught me to learn to love
a woman from the inside out."

Some Women

They are like drunken monarchs
a crooked zig zaggity journey here and a
descending fluttering sideways flight there.
To admonish them is to kill
that which makes them
beautiful.

Sleeping Dogs

When it is quiet
with no noise of dissension
why seek defiance?

When it is quiet
with no sound of deception
why hunt damnation?

When it is quiet
with no noise of divergence
why wake destruction?

When it is quiet
remain still and breathe.

Reincarnation

When my ash is toss
with prayer and a
cross I will return as
a shaman dressed as an
anchorman. Call me Dan.
When placed in soft ground
I will emerge from soil
to toil and paint blue flowers
in oil. Call me Earl.
When I pass below green grass
I will return as a six string trick.
Call me Dick. When I stray
from mortal eyes I will defy
the laws of man and return
as ruler of my clan. Call me Khan.
When I die and my spirit is set free,
I will remain to cherish what was me.
When I go as autumn leaves blow
I will return. I will return.

Live Bravely

when the world presents
a veneer no more pleasant
than a wiccan's sneer.

Live Courageously

when the lame
keep playing the
same blaming game.

Live Heroically

when global indifference
weakens one's humanitarian
perseverance.

Live Boldly

when love's heartache
bears a physical body ache.

Live Valiantly

when the demise of a friend
comes without warning
or a compromise.

Live Daringly

when the world vilifies
and crucifies your naivety.

Utmost, Live Fearlessly

when you surmise the person
you are is not the character

you wanted to be. For in a
land where there is no war
people wage their own.

Live Bravely

Time

It does not stay for those with rouge
how can it remain for a scrooge?
It sheds no tears for a star
how can it cry for a dwarf?
It holds not for the gentry
why would it keep for the elementary?
Unless held between friends
impermanence is the cornerstone of time.

Definitive Thoughts

There are only so many times I will ever make love.
Have I really made love, or has intimacy distanced me?

There are only so many times I will ever sleep.
Are my pillows comfortable and have I gotten a good night's rest?

There are only so many times I will ever eat.
Have I eaten what I wanted or has my dish been a stale palate?

There are only so many times I will ever have to see.
Have I seen what I wanted
or have I viewed the world through a colored screen?

There are only so many times I will ever have to laugh.
Have I really laughed or has the joke been on me?

There are only so many times I will ever have to talk.
Have I told my friends I care or have I meant to say what I have not said?

There is only so much time I will ever have to live.
Have I used my time wisely or has father time used me?

Pygmy Intellectualism

There is wear and tear on your once new car but there is no climate change.

Pharmaceutical companies and opiates are the cause of people's addiction but the NRA and guns are not the cause of our bullet affliction.

Your fiancée should love you for who you are but a wedding ring should cost how many month's salary?

We cry racism as we march but forget young boys wearing blue or red kill their own kind as much as whites kill blacks.

They say immigration takes jobs from true Americans, I say how many of you have ever seen a true American pick a fruit or vegetable from anywhere else but from a plate or a bowl?

For many of us, getting justice from an injustice caught on video is not plausible, blessed are you who receive vindication for a probable bad deed committed thirty years ago. We say, "us too".

Many believe only blacks receive welfare, I wonder who receives it in West Virginia?

There is wear and tear on your once strong bones but there is no damage to the ozone.

There is no gun violence.

And there is no lying by God fearing law abiding citizens there are just alternative facts.

www.ingramcontent.com/pod-product-compliance
Lightning Source LLC
Chambersburg PA
CBHW052117110526
44592CB00013B/1646